EViLUTiON: THE TROOF

This book has been specially written and
published for World Book Day 2011.
For further information please see
www.worldbookday.com

World Book Day in the UK and Ireland
is made possible by generous sponsorship
from National Book Tokens, participating
publishers, authors and booksellers.
Booksellers who accept the £1 World
Book Day Token bear the full cost
of redeeming it.

To celebrate World Book Day,
Orchard Books are offering 25% off all
the fantastic Jiggy McCue books by
Michael Lawrence!

The Killer Underpants
The Toilet of Doom
The Meanest Genie
The Snottle
The Curse of the Poltergoose
Nudie Dudie
Neville the Devil
Ryan's Brain
The Iron, the Switch and the Broom Cupboard
Kid Swap
One for All and All for Lunch
Rudie Dudie

And the new Jiggy's Genes series:
Jiggy's Magic Balls
Jiggy the Vampire Slayer

To claim your discount just go to
www.orchardbooks.co.uk/jiggymccue
Fill your basket with Jiggy books then
enter the promotional code **Jiggy25** at
the checkout!

A JIGGY McCUE STORY

EViLUTiON:
THE TROOF

MICHAEL LAWRENCE

ORCHARD BOOKS

Visit Michael Lawrence's website:
www.wordybug.com

And find loads of Jiggy fun at:
www.jiggymccue.com

ORCHARD BOOKS
338 Euston Road, London NW1 3BH
Orchard Books Australia
Level 17/207 Kent Street, Sydney, NSW 2000

First published in the UK in 2011

ISBN 978 0 95662 767 4

A CIP catalogue recocsrd for this book is available from
the British Library.

Printed and bound in Great Britain by CPI Bookmarque,
Croydon CR0 4TD

The text paper within this book was donated by Abitibi Consolidated
and Paper Management Services Ltd

1 3 5 7 9 10 8 6 4 2

Printed in Great Britain

Orchard Books is a division of Hachette Children's Books,
an Hachette UK company.

www.hachette.co.uk

CHAPTER ONE

McCue's the name. Jiggy McCue. I'm called Jiggy because jigging's what I do in times of stress. Which means I jig a lot. So what happens to stress me out so much? I'll tell you. It's being chased by a dead goose. It's being victimised by a six-hundred-year-old genie. It's being out in public when all your clothes disappear. It's having your life (and crotch) taken over by underpants with a power complex. It's…

But you get the picture.

Stuff like that happens to me so often that I sometimes worry about getting out of bed in the morning. Well, wouldn't you, when you have no idea what's waiting the other side of the door to kick you in the fruit and nuts? I mention this to prepare you for the utterly unbelievable thing that happened on a school trip recently. This time it didn't just happen to me, though. It also happened to Eejit Atkins, who as well as being in my class at Ranting Lane School is my next door neighbour on the Brook Farm Estate. And there's something else you should know about Atkins.

You know in the stories of Robin Hood there's this character called Little John? They call him Little John because he's taller than everyone else. It's a joke. Ha-ha. Well, I'd like to say that Atkins is called Eejit for a joke too, because he's a genius. But it wouldn't be true. Eejit's as thick as a rhino's backside. Here's an example of a typical Atkins-McCue chat.

'Jig,' he says, coming up to me.

'Yes?' I say.

'You know that thing?' he says.

'What thing?' I say.

'That thing,' he says.

'Oh, that thing,' I say, without the faintest idea what he's on about.

'Yeah,' he says.

Then there's this long pause while he stares blankly into space.

'What about it?' I say eventually to stop the suspense killing me.

'What about what?' he says, glancing at me.

'That thing,' I say.

'What thing?' he says.

'The thing you just asked me if I knew.'

'Dunno what you're talkin' about,' he says, and scoots off.

And that was one of our sharper conversations.

Anyway. The deal with Atkins occurred on this outing to the Eversledge-Hope Museum of Natural History, which no one in our class had heard of till then. 'What's an eversledge-hope when it's at home, sir?' Elvis Bisley asked Mr Rice on the bus that took us there.

It was a surprise to find Rice on the bus. He usually lurks in the gym or on the sports field, but there he was, still in the stupid red tracksuit he wears at all times, even in Assembly.

'Probably the same as when it's on holiday!' he answered with a witty shout.

Mr Rice always shouts. Apart from blowing whistles and lobbing balls into giant hairnets, shouting's what he does best. His shouts were quieter than usual today though. The reason, we decided, was that our other minder — a science teacher called Mrs Baldeagle — could shout for Eurovision, and he was scared of her. Mrs B didn't take our class for Science, and none of us sobbed too uncontrollably about that because she reminded us of Hitler, only without the joke tash and stiff arm.

'When did you last go to a museum, sir?' Marlene Bronson asked Mr Rice, like she cared.

'It's been a while!' he shouted softly in reply.

'Come on, when?' said Bronson, who doesn't like to let a thing go once she's sunk her manky teeth into it. 'When you were forty, say?'

'Forty?!' said Rice. 'How old d'you think I am, for Dawkins' sake?!'

'Well, you're older than my dad.'

'How old's your dad?'

'Hundred and two,' said Hislop.

Bronson leant over and thumped him. Bronson likes thumping boys. It's her hobby. Hislop yelled in pain.

'QUIET BACK THERE!'

That was Mrs Baldeagle, from the front of the bus. Mr Rice hunched down with the rest of us near the back.

'Keep it down, you lot,' he hissed.

We might have kept it down too – for a minute or three – if this ear-gutting semi-musical thing hadn't suddenly erupted nearby.

'What is that dreadful *racket*?!' Mr Rice gasped.

'It's me new ringtone,' said Eejit Atkins, waving a mobile phone I'd never seen before. 'I wrote it meself.'

'Mobiles aren't permitted during schooltime,' said Skinner, who's just got to become a teacher when he grows up, the toad.

'Why don't you put us out of our misery and answer it?' I asked Eejit.

'I'm just testin' me ringtone,' he said. 'Cool, innit?'

'Cool?' I said. 'No, Atkins, it's not cool. It's nothing like cool. It's a million miles short of cool, and it cannot be allowed to live.'

'How could anyone write a tune so tune-*less*?' said Fiala Kolinski.

'No one but Atkins would even *want* to write something like that,' said another girl. Eejit's not popular with girls for some reason.

'Mr Atkins!' Mr Rice said. 'Turn it off! Now!'

'FOR THE LAST TIME BE QUIET AT THE BACK!' bawled Mrs Baldeagle from the front.

Mr Rice hunkered down again. 'Please?' he begged Atkins.

'Oh, awright.'

Eejit stuck his bottom lip out and punched buttons on his mobile.

The horrible ringtone went on.

He punched more buttons.

It went on. And on. And on.

All around him, ears were clasped, mouths were groaned, eyes were rolled. Mrs Baldeagle and the kids in the very front seats showed no sign of hearing the ringtone, but the rest of us couldn't miss it.

'How come you can put a personalised ringtone on your phone but don't know how to stop it?' Angie Mint wanted to know.[*]

'The man at the car boot only showed me how to make a tone,' Eejit said.

'Car boot? You got it from a car boot?'

'Yeh. It were cheap.'

'I don't care how cheap it was,' said Angie. 'If you don't turn it off within two seconds, it's following your head through the window.'

Eejit hit the buttons again, but the horrible ringtone still didn't stop.

'Oh, give it here!'

Angie snatched the phone off him and started on the buttons, hoping to find the one

---

[*] Angie's one of my best mates. It's not her fault that she's a girl.

that would turn it off. She failed. But suddenly she stopped buttoning, and smirked.

'You want to know why this was so cheap, Atkins?'

'Why?'

'The maker's name. One of the letters is wrong.'

She held the phone up for him to see the manufacturer's name.

NOGIA.

'Which letter?' said Atkins.

Everyone was chortling at this when Angie's jaw dropped. She was staring at the back of the phone, eyes on stalks.

'Jig…'

She leant over. Showed me the four tiny little words she'd found.

A LITTLE DEVILS PRODUCT

My throat went dry. So did my palms, and quite a few other places. I'd come across Little Devils products before and hoped I'd never see another. And here I was, inches from one on a school bus.*

'Get that thing away from me!' I hissed.

---

* To find out about Jiggy's previous run-ins with Little Devils you'll have to read *The Killer Underpants*, *Neville the Devil*, *Nudie Dudie*, and *Rudie Dudie*. Sorry.

As Angie handed the phone back to Atkins it stopped ringing, even though no one had found the off button. Whews of relief all round. The grateful unclasping of ears, ungroaning of mouths, unrolling of eyes.

'Mind of its own, that thing,' someone said.

'More than its owner has,' said someone else.

'You better not get calls on that while I'm about,' I said to Eejit.

'No chance,' he said. 'No one knows me number.'

'Well do me a favour, don't spread it around.'

'I can't. I don't know it meself.'

With normal service just about resumed, Pete Garrett asked Mr Rice why he was there.

'I've often wondered that,' I said. '"Why is Mr Rice here?", I say. "I mean what is the *point* of him?"'

'Don't push your luck just cos we're out of school, McCue,' Rice shouted – quietly so he wouldn't get yelled at by Mrs Baldeagle.

'I never had any to push,' I said, which was very true.

'I mean today, with us,' said Pete to the Ricicle. 'I mean we're going to a science-type museum, and Mr Flowerdew's our Science teacher and he was supposed to take us, and he isn't here, and you are, so why?'

'Mr Flowerdew's in meltdown,' Rice said.

'Meltdown?'

'His gas bill arrived this morning. He had to go to the doctor for emergency medication.'

'And you took his place because you were the only teacher not doing anything useful?' said Harry Potter.*

'How would you like a detention, Potter?' asked Mr Rice.

'Ooh, yes please, sir, I live for detentions.'

A round of applause for that (we're so easy to please).

'I WON'T TELL YOU AGAIN!' screamed Baldeagle from the front.

When the bus eventually drew up outside the Eversledge-Hope Museum of Natural History, Mrs B stood up and ordered us off. When we were all standing on the pavement she told us to get in twos and stay with our partners.

'We ain't got no partners,' someone said.

'WELL, *CHOOSE* SOME!' bawled our personal Hitler in drag.

When everyone started scratching their

---

* Yes, there's a boy in my class called Harry Potter. He spends a lot of time trying to live it down – the name, not being in my class.

heads wondering how to go about choosing partners, Mrs Baldeagle grabbed the nearest shoulder and slammed it against the next nearest and pushed the owners towards the museum steps.

'GO INSIDE AND WAIT IN AN ORDERLY FASHION!'

The first pair of partners went up the steps curling their lips at one another and Miss partnered two more, then two more, and two more. I was one of those who got a partner he wouldn't have chosen in three lifetimes.

'No, Miss,' I protested. 'Anyone but Atkins.'

But she wasn't listening. She was too busy choosing the wrong partners for everyone else.

We partnered ones were mooching up the museum steps when our unhappy mutterings were interrupted by a tall ginger-bearded man standing by the doors.

'Do not be fooled!' he bawled. 'It didn't happen the way they tell you in there! I, Remus P. Haversack, have dedicated my working life to unearthing the true causes and spurs of evolutionary change. Read my self-published work, "Evolution: the Truth", available from my website, www.evoltrue.com. Take a leaflet, read more!'

'SILENCE!'

No prizes for guessing who that was. The ginger man shut his beardy trap along with the rest of us. But as we passed him he pressed leaflets into a few hands, including mine.

'What's evilution, Jig?' Atkins asked as we went into the museum.

'Don't you remember Mr Flowerdew wasting weeks of our lives explaining it to prepare us for today?' I said, stuffing the mad scientist's flyer into a jacket pocket.

'No.'

'Well, you were there. Your body was anyway.'

'But it's about evil, right?'

'No, Atkins, it's not about evil. It's e-*vol*-ution, not e-*vil*-ution. It's about turning from ape to person. You've got a way to go with that. Look, kid, just cos we've been paired off, don't feel that you have to talk to me, OK? In fact, feel free to keep as far away from me as possible today.'

'Evil,' Atkins said. His little eyes were shining. 'Cool.'

My wise words had gone right over his head, probably because the top of it only came up to my armpit. I sighed. It was starting to feel like a long day, and it had only just begun.

CHAPTER TWO

'OK, we've done the museum, can we go now?' said Bryan Ryan as the last of us strolled through the doors.

'QUIET!!!' screamed Mrs Baldeagle, almost turning three museum staff to quivering dust. They didn't look like they were used to big ladies with faces like giant rock cakes and eyes like goat droppings. (There was nothing about Baldeagle that said, 'I'm a nice gentle person deep down, let's talk about our favourite things and sip milkshakes together.') When she started herding us kids from room to room the staff kept well back. Mr Rice looked like he wished he could stay out of range too. I almost felt sorry for him. Almost. He was Mr Rice, after all.

A lot of the stuff we were pointed at interested us about as much as Baldeagle's knicker size, but some of the stuffed animals weren't so bad, and the dinosaur skeletons were quite cool. Lots of bones and teeth, dinosaurs. There were a couple of small disturbances in the 'Meet the Relatives' room, which had all these fragments of flint and things, and scenes behind glass panels containing primitive people with nothing on. Most of the prims were just standing there, like they were waiting for the first nudist bus to be invented, but a few were in walking poses, all bent over like they had back trouble, and some were sitting around looking thoroughly cheesed off. There was a fair bit of chat about this lot.

'What did they *do* all day back then?'

'Look for clothes shops, probably.'

'Must've been hell without TV.'

'Or Xboxes.'

'Or iPads.'

'Who's Charles Darlin'?' Atkins asked when he heard the name in an audio commentary he'd attached to his ear.

'Doesn't that kid listen to *anything* in class?' Nafeesa Aslam said.

'He can't remember being in class,' said Julia Frame.

I noticed Ryan gazing at a long board headed

'Evolutionary Timeline' which showed how life had developed from the very beginning. I checked it out too. 'Hey, Bry-Ry,' I said, 'four hundred million years ago you had fins. I always knew there was something fishy about you.'

But he was reading. Ryan can't read and listen at the same time. He's a footballer.

'It says here that all living things are related to one another,' said Milo Dakin, clocking another board nearby.

'I wouldn't be related to you if you paid me,' said Marlene Bronson.

'Don't worry, I wouldn't,' Milo said. 'But you're related to me, like it or not. Me and a mushroom.'

'A mushroom?'

'Me, a mushroom, a moth, a caterpillar and a cow.'

'Who you callin' a cow, Dakin?'

'No, you're *related* to a cow. Look.'

'I don't want to look,' said Marlene.

'What cow's she related to?' someone asked.

'Not a *particular* cow,' Milo said. 'All cows. And dogs. So next time someone calls you a dog, Bronson, they won't be far wrong.'

Marlene started towards him, but I and a few others surged between them for a gander at Milo's board. It was true, we were related to each other and mushrooms and cows and dogs, and quite a few other things.

'Who thinks we're descended from monkeys?' one girl asked from another part of the room.

'Atkins definitely is,' said another girl.

'Atkins isn't descended from monkeys, he is one,' said a third.

'Uh, uh, uh,' said Eejit, bouncing up and down and scratching his armpits. I worry about that boy, I really do.

'We're not descended from them, though,' the first girl said. 'Monkeys and humans share a common ancestor, which means we're cousins.'

'Everyone knows that,' said Julia Frame.

'Do we? Oh, I thought it sounded familiar.'

'Uh, uh, uh,' said Eejit, still bouncing and scratching the Atkins pits.

'WHO IS MAKING THAT *RIDICULOUS* NOISE?!' screamed Mrs Baldeagle. She couldn't see the culprit because he was behind the bunch of us checking out the display boards.

'Atkins!' half a dozen loyal classmates shouted.

'WHICH ONE'S ATKINS?!'

Eejit put the lid on the chimp impression and squatted down so he stood even less chance of being spotted.

'Can't see him, Miss,' I said, 'but I just discovered that I'm his cousin.'

Milo Dakin grinned. 'So am I.'

And then the ball was rolling.

'And me.'

'And me.'

'And me.'

'So's Marlene,' said Angie.

'YOU'RE ALL *COUSINS*?' said Mrs B in amazement.

'Yeah, we're just one big unhappy family,' said Pete.

Baldeagle looked like she half believed it too, which suggested that we might be able to squeeze a drop more juice out of her than we'd expected, but before we could get started a tweedy man in a bow tie said something to her and she clapped her hands and told us that he was going to talk to us, and that if we wanted to see another sunset we'd better give him our undivided attention.

'I wouldn't wanna meet him in no dark alley,' Atkins said to me.

At first I thought he meant Bow Tie Man, but he chinned a gloomy cave behind a big glass panel. There were five life-size ancestor types in the cave plus one modern gent, also life-size. The modern one wore overalls and was on his knees brushing bits into a dustpan. The others weren't doing anything, mainly because they weren't alive. Two of the ancestor types were kids, but it was the third lifeless adult that Eejit had chinned. He sat on a rock outside the cave like he wanted nothing to do with the family group. He was darker than them, and not as hairy, and he had these big scowly eyebrows and eyes like jet that seemed to be trying to stare us out.

'He remind you of anyone?' I asked Eejit.

'Him?' he said, as the man with the dustpan and brush slipped out of a door beside the display.

'No, the one you wouldn't want to meet in a dark alley. He could be Baldeagle's long-lost uncle.'

'Baldeagle's lost her uncle?'

'No, I mean…' I sighed. 'Forget it.'

'PAY ATTENTION EVERYONE!' Mrs Baldeagle bellowed.

About three-quarters of the class turned to face the tweedy museum staffer who'd landed the sweet job of talking to us.

'I'm here today,' he began, 'to tell you about human evolution and—'

'SPEAK UP!' barked batty Baldeagle.

The man ducked like she'd taken a swipe at his head. But then he straightened his bow tie and spoke up as ordered.

'As I'm sure you're aware, we humans are a very recent evolutionary development. What you might not know is that we're just one of over two hundred primate species living on Earth today. Over the past sixty-five million years or so, many primates flourished for a time, then died out and—'

'I'm bored,' said Eejit Atkins.

'You're going to get a lot boreder,' I told him. 'He's just warming up.'

I was right about that. The man from the museum droned on and on, and soon feet were shuffling like they were all trying to learn a different dance, and there were an awful lot of sighs. I even saw Mr Rice stifle a yawn.

'We humans are known as Homo sapiens,' the museum man said, 'which is Latin for 'wise man' or 'knowing man'. We have very highly developed brains—'

'Not all of us,' said Skinner, glancing at Atkins.

'—capable of reason, organised speech and problem solving. This mental ability, combined with manual dexterity, allows us to—'

I went into a trance. I wasn't the only one. There were quite a lot of blank expressions. I don't know how long my trance went on for, but then I realised the man's voice had stopped and Baldeagle was shouting that it was time to move to the next part of the museum.

''Bout time,' I said, glancing down at Atkins. 'All this standing still isn't good for the—'

I stopped because he was even more vacant than usual. Vacant as in not there. As the class moved out, pushing and shoving, thumping and pinching, I hung back, looking for Eejit. No sign of him.

But then I noticed something.

In the artificial cave behind the glass there were now three primitive kids instead of two.

All three stood absolutely still, staring blankly out like they were posing for a camera.

One of them wore Ranting Lane school uniform.

CHAPTER THREE

I waited for the last of my classmates to leave the room, then put my face against the glass and mouthed 'Atkins, you plank, come out of there'. He didn't move. Didn't even blink. I knew what that meant. Eejit can freeze like an icicle when he wants to. When we were younger and he got massacred in shoot-outs and plastic sword fights, he could stay dead till bedtime. Looking at him in that cave it was like he'd become a model of himself. If you didn't know him and he hadn't been wearing the uniform you wouldn't have paid him any more attention than the two other primitive ape kids in there.

I glanced at the door next to the display. It was ever-so-slightly ajar. My class and minders were gone now, so I reckoned that if I was quick…

I darted through the door.

'Atkins!' I hissed from the side of the display.

He still didn't move.

'If you don't come out,' I said, 'I'm having you stuffed and put in here permanently.'

Not a twitch.

I gritted the McCue teeth and stepped into the cave.

It felt weird in there. Gloomier than it looked from the other side of the glass. The primitive people were more lifelike up close, and the scowling one, the more human-seeming one, looked like he might turn on you at any moment and thump you. But I didn't have time to marvel at how real they seemed.

'I just don't believe you, Atkins,' I said, grabbing one of his ears.

'Leave it out, Jig.' He jerked his ear out of my grip. 'I just wanted to see what it was like being a model, is all.'

'Well now you know, so let's get out of here.'

'Hang on.' He whipped out the mobile phone from the car boot. 'Take me picture with these two, willya?'

I glanced nervously out through the glass. Fresh visitors could come into the room on the other side of it at any moment.

'There's no *time*!' I said.

But urgency was one of the many things Eejit wasn't good at.

'No, hold on,' he said, 'I just got to find the button what turns it—'

That was as far as he got before the horrible ringtone started again. I slapped my forehead.

'Atkins! Shut that thing off!'

'I'm tryin', I'm tryin',' he said, punching buttons like a maniac.

'Oh, give it to me!'

I reached for the phone – yes, even though it was a Little Devils product, the last thing in the universe that someone called McCue should get within a continent of. I grabbed it, but Atkins wouldn't let go, so right away we were struggling for control of it.

And in the struggle…we dropped it.

Unfortunately, the dropping didn't stop the ringing. Anything but. It sent it into tuneless overdrive and an even higher pitch. I pounced. So did Eejit. Our heads crunched. We gasped, staggered, but held on to the phone. Head throbbing, brain swirling, eyes watering, I glimpsed Atkins looking even more dazed than usual. But he still wouldn't let go of the phone. Nor would I. Only when the ringtone suddenly stopped of its own accord did I let go of it. It was a relief to be able to concentrate on clearing my head and stopping my feet trying to walk in different directions. As I got a handle on these things, I found some new things to think about. Things like why the five life-size primitives weren't there any more. Or the glass panel. Or the museum on the other side of it.

'Uh?' said Eejit, who'd also noticed these differences.

We were staring at a desert that went on forever. And the cave we were in wasn't an artificial one. It was real.

'I don't get it,' I said.

'Me neither,' said Atkins. 'But the sky's nice.'

He was right about that. It was nice. Very blue. Hardly a cloud in it. The sky outside the museum had been grey. Full of rain getting ready to soak people without umbrellas. This sky looked like it had never heard of rain.

'When's lunch?' Eejit asked.

'Lunch?'

'I'm starving.'

'Atkins,' I said. 'A minute ago we were with our class in a museum of natural history, and suddenly we're alone in a desert, and you're thinking about food?'

'A person's gotta eat,' he said.

I shook my head in amazement. It must be nice being Eejit Atkins. Something utterly banana-shaped occurs and instead of wondering about it he turns his piddle-quality mind to fodder. But me? I could only gape, at the cave we were in so suddenly, at all that open space outside it, at the seven hairy nude ape people loping along…

'Do you see what I see?' I asked Atkins.

'I dunno, what do you see?'

'Seven hairy nude ape people, loping.'

'Yeah, that's what I see.'

'I hate to say it,' I said, 'but this looks awfully like your actual primitive times. The early days of man. And woman. And kid.'

Now you might think that in a situation like this I'd say something like, 'Oh, I must be dreaming'. But like I said at the beginning, unnatural stuff happens to me all the time, so I hardly ever think I'm dreaming. Even when I'm really dreaming something wacky my sleeping self says, 'Hey, come on, pull the one in the middle.' But this…this was a bit off the chart even for me, and as I saw it I had two choices.

Choice 1. Spend the next half hour trying to make sense of things.
Choice 2. Say, 'OK, so this is early human history, live with it.'

Tap-tap. Tap-tap-tap. Tap-tap-tap-tap-tap.
'What's that?' said Eejit.
'Sounds like tapping,' I said.
I leant out of the cave to see what was doing the tapping and saw a man in what looked like a cheap ape costume from the Cheap Ape Costume Hire Shop. He was just as nude as the seven desert lopers, but not as hairy, and he was darker, and more fierce-looking, and he was tapping a rock with a long bone that could once have belonged to a man-sized leg.

'It's the one what give me the creeps,' said Eejit.

He was almost right. The bone-wielder wasn't Mrs Baldeagle's long-lost uncle's double, but there was a likeness. I was thinking this when Eejit's phone rang yet again. The ringtone had gone back to its tuneless original, but even that was ten times worse than bad enough.

'Eejit, will you stop that?' I said.

'I don't know *how*,' he said.

'Well do something. Anything. Jump on it, smash it against a rock, or your head, I don't care, but be quick or we could have ourselves an audience we could do without.'

It was too late, of course. The ape people might not have been tremendously well stocked in the grey matter department but their ears worked. The seven heads of the desert lopers turned our way and their fourteen hands reached for every one of their ears. The nearer ape, though, the darker one, he didn't cover his ears. No, he stood up, threw his head back, and…howled.

'Done it,' said Eejit, magically finding the ringtone's off button.

'You have,' I said.

While the lighter ape people uncovered their ears and went back to their nude loping, the darker one dropped his leg bone and came towards us – walking more upright than you'd expect from someone in a suit like that.

'See those shadows?' I said to Atkins, pointing to the back of the cave. 'I think we could do a lot worse than merge with them in a hurry.'

He didn't catch on right away – of course he didn't, he wasn't called Eejit for nothing – but when he realised how close the apeman was he shoved me aside and scampered into the shadows at speed. I wasn't far behind him. Only when we could no longer see the end of each other's noses did we feel safe.

'Jig? You there?'

'Quiet. We don't want him to hear us.'

Pause.

Another pause.

A third pause.

Then…

'Erg!' That was Eejit.

'What do you mean, "erg"?' That was me.

'Why have you grabbed me throat?'

'Grabbed your throat? I haven't grabbed your – erg!'

There was a hand round mine too. The kind of hand that wants you to know that it might not be the best idea you ever had to try and make a break for it.

And then we were being hauled (by the neck) towards the light. Only when the apeman had stood us outside the cave did he let go of our throats. He looked pretty unhappy with us but he didn't say anything, just looked us up and down like we were an entirely new species – which I suppose we were, to him. It was kind of hard to know what to do next, so I switched on the charm that works so well with really old people and nuns.

'Hi. My name's Jiggy, this is my friend Eejit, and you are…?'

'Grunt.'

'Grunt? OK, cool. Now listen, Grunt, sorry if Eejit's mobile disturbed the old rock tapping routine, but—'

I'd snatched the phone from Atkins to show our new friend what I was talking about, but Grunt had wasted no time in snatching it off me in turn, and now he was fingering it like Eejit had been doing a few minutes ago. And then the horrible ringtone started once more.

'Hey, Grunt ol' pal,' I said, 'do us a favour. Hand that to my friend here. With any luck, sometime in the next millennium or two he'll hit the off button again.'

But Grunt didn't give the phone back. He smiled, like he knew something we didn't. And perhaps he did, because, while the ringtone went on and on, he began to change. I don't mean physically. He went on looking pretty much the same, but something must have happened inside him, in his head, because...hard to explain, but his attitude became just a bit more human. Not so human that I had an overpowering urge to sit down with him and swap jokes, but there was a definite humanisation thing going on there.

And then he did something amazing. He looked from one to the other of us, raised a finger to make sure we saw it, and brought it down on one of the phone's buttons like he was showing us how to do it – and the ringtone stopped.

'He's smarter than he looks,' I said to Eejit. 'Smarter than some others I could mention within spitting distance.'

'Which button was that?' Eejit asked Grunt.

Grunt pulled the phone to his chest like he was saying 'Get your own, it's mine.' Then he spun around and strode away.

'Here, me Nogia!' Eejit shouted. Grunt

carried on walking. 'He's nicked it,' Eejit said in disbelief.

'Maybe he always wanted a mobile,' I said. 'I bet there's a lot of apes he'll want to call as soon as one of them sets up a network.'

'I'm goin' after him.'

He took a step forward. I gripped his puny bicep.

'Eejit. Think about it. Here we are in...' – I looked about me, couldn't think what to call it – '...wherever, which I'm guessing might not be staggeringly friendly to advanced life forms like us – well, me – so maybe we should be careful whose footsteps we walk in.'

'I want me phone,' he said.

'Yes, I get that, but our new chum has it, and he has this way with bones and rocks, and grabbing necks and all, so maybe we should sort of, you know, not mess with him too much. Eh? Whaddayasay?'

'I want me phone back.'

And off he went, after Grunt.

I glanced back at the shadowy cave, which looked pretty cosy to me all of a sudden, and sighed. Here I was in BC zero-zero-zero-times-whatever-plus-zero, and I had no choice but to follow Eejit Atkins on the heels of a naked apeman who'd swiped the mobile phone he got cheap at a car boot sale. His Little Devils phone.

Did I mention that my life isn't always totally normal?

CHAPTER FOUR

Grunt had a long stride, so we were still way behind him when he stepped into a grove of trees. We didn't go in after him, just peered between the trunks. There were about two dozen apemen in there, same species as Grunt, though more hunched over, like he was when we first saw him. Most of them sat around picking things out of their body hair and eating whatever they found in there.*

Grunt wasn't doing that. He was making weird mouth sounds, like he was trying to start a conversation, but he didn't seem to be getting anywhere. A few looked his way, but most of them ignored him.

'I wonder what he thinks he's saying?' I whispered to Atkins.

'He's telling them to listen up cos he's got news for them,' he replied.

'Good guess,' I said as Grunt started jumping up and down in what looked pretty

---

* The primitive man version of salted peanuts maybe.

much like ape rage.

'It's not a guess, it's what he's saying. And now he's losing it cos they ain't paying no attention.'

I stared at him. 'Are you telling me that you can *understand* him?'

'Yeah, course.'

'What do you mean "yeah, course"? Eejit, he's an apeman, and you're human, near enough. You're not supposed to speak ape.'

He shrugged like it was just one of those things he could do. Then he said, 'He's heard us.'

I looked back into the clearing. Grunt was heading our way. I would have suggested that we kick dust, but before my lips could flare into action Grunt was with us. Holding out Eejit's mobile.

'Grunt, grunt, grunty-grunt-grunt,' said Grunt.

Atkins grinned. 'He wants to hear me ringtone! Well at least someone likes it.'

He took the phone, fingered a button, and the nightmare ringtone started again. It had just occurred to me to ask why the button that turned it on didn't also turn it off when Grunt snatched the phone and stalked back into the clearing with it.

'He's nicked it again,' Eejit said.

'He has,' I said. 'But don't go after him this time, eh? Let's just see what happens next.'

We watched through the trees as Grunt held the insanely ringing phone in the air. The others gawped at it like it was the strangest thing they'd ever seen or heard, which it probably was, and as they gawped they shivered, like they'd just woken from a deep sleep. Then the ones that were sitting or squatting got to their feet and stood very upright, and the ones that were already standing threw their shoulders back and stood straighter than before. And their faces became more intelligent. Not hugely intelligent, but they could almost have given Atkins a run for his money, and their eyes, which had looked kind of dull, were brighter now, and staring around like they were seeing things for the very first time.

'Woh,' I said. 'If we're not witnessing speeded-up evolution I don't know what it is.'

'Evilution...' Atkins said, like he thought he'd heard that word before somewhere. 'So they're evil then, yeh?'

I sighed. 'No. Listen. I explained that. It's e-*vol*-ution. E-*vol*-ution. Nothing to do with evil.'

But he'd already tuned out. All his feeble attention was on what was going on in the clearing. On Grunt stabbing the phone with a finger, just once, and the ringtone immediately stopping. He couldn't get over the fact that Grunt knew where the off button was. I was impressed too. In less time than it takes to scrape one of my mother's disgusting excuses for a meal into the waste bin, Grunt had graduated from rock tapping to turning a Little Devils phone off. Some of the apemen peered at the suddenly silent phone. A couple reached for it, but Grunt smacked their fingers. That smack said it all. He wasn't just one of them any more. He was their leader.

The Boss.

Suddenly, out of the blue-blue sky, I remembered the man on the museum steps a few hundred thousand years in the future, and the flyer he'd pressed into my hand. I pulled the crumpled piece of paper from my pocket and read it.

The Conclusions of Remus P. Haversack, Evolutionist.

Darwin described evolution as a continuous process of change over time, but a lifetime's dedicated investigation has led me to a very different conclusion: that it was the planet itself that instigated the great evolutionary changes – with the power of sound. Yes, sound and sound alone, fired from the world's core at irregular intervals throughout Earth's long history; sound waves of such pitch and timbre as to alter the balance and quality of life on the surface. It was not meteors, earthquakes or climate change that destroyed the dinosaurs, but sound. It was not 'natural selection' that advanced the brains of our early ancestors. It was sound. For the full story, read **Evolution: the Truth**, signed copies available from www.evoltrue.com

Sound could do such things? No. Impossible. Cats would bark sooner. But what if the lanky ginger beardy on the steps was right? What if certain kinds of sound had caused all the big evolutionary changes? If so, maybe it wasn't only sounds from *inside* the planet that could get things buzzing. Maybe the right sort of sound from other sources could also flip a switch in primitive brains to boot their owners a bunch of rungs up the evolutionary ladder. If that was it, and the outrageous ringtone had pulled this off, it hadn't done much for the paler primitives, the desert lopers. Maybe it would take another kind of sound to spark their brains, or they would evolve naturally, or not at all. But the apes in the clearing, well, Eejit's personalised ringtone had certainly done a job on them – specially Grunt, who, because he'd heard it three times now, was a heap smarter than the rest.

But none of that explained how the two of us had been transferred from the artificial cave in the museum to an actual cave way back. Maybe that was the awful ringtone's doing too. Eejit's phone was a Little Devils product, after all, and Little Devils products are capable of anything and can't be second-guessed. Not by me anyway.

I was mulling on all this when Grunt glanced towards our trees and grunted at the nearest apemen. When they grunted back he grunted again – more fiercely – and they headed our way.

'We'd better go,' I said.

'But he's still got me Nogia,' Eejit said.

'Never mind that.'

I gripped his arm and set off at a run with it and the rest of him. We didn't get far before Grunt's heavies overtook us and flipped us round.

'Hi,' I said with a boyish smile.*

'Grunt-grunt-gruntity-grunt.'

'They want us to go back with them,' said Eejit.

Back in the clearing they stood us in front of their dear leader, who gazed at us silently for so long that I began to get nervous and started to jig. He looked at my legs and twitchy arms like they'd gone crazy.

'Sorry,' I said. 'Can't help it. It's a condition. You probably don't get it in the year dot.'

Grunt didn't answer, just carried on looking.

'Eejit,' I said out of the side of my mouth, 'ask him what he wants before I tango out of here without a partner.'

'How do I do that?' he asked.

'How? You flap the Atkins cake-hole and toss some words his way, how else?'

'But I don't speak his lingo.'

---

* I'm really good at those. It's a boy thing.

'I thought you did.'

'No, I just understand it, is all.'

'Pity. I was hoping you could persuade him to make the building of schools a criminal offence for all time, or at least ban teachers.'

But when he was ready, Grunt made it pretty clear why he'd wanted us brought back. He'd had a vision, you see. A vision of Eejit and me tied to a boulder in front of the cave with strips of bendy wood.

'I guess no one's invented rope yet,' I said as we were tied to a boulder in front of the cave with strips of bendy wood. 'Any clue what this is about?'

'Well, I heard them say something about looking forward to the next meal,' Eejit said.

'And that's it? Nothing about us being invited to this meal?'

'Don't think so. There was a bit of whispering behind their hands, though, like they had this secret.'

'You know,' I said, 'that might not be the greatest news you ever failed to hear.'

While we were waiting to see if we were going to be early man's idea of a fish supper with an extra portion of chips, Grunt got something organised in the cave. Twisting our heads almost all the way round, we saw him climb one of the bumpy walls and place Eejit's phone on a high ledge. Jumping down he grunted at his mates, who looked at one another like the chief had lost his brain cell. Their reaction seemed to annoy Grunt a tad, because his next round of grunts sounded like a primitive hissy fit.

'Did you get that?' I asked Eejit.

'Yes. He's telling them to get down on their knees.'

'Why? What for?'

But he didn't need to answer this. I saw for myself. The apemen fell to the ground, stuck their backsides in the air, and bowed very low – to worship Eejit Atkins's mobile phone.

CHAPTER FIVE

Atkins and I were still strapped to the boulder when Grunt's men suddenly stopped airing their rear ends, jumped up, and dived into the shadows. I would have done that too if I could've. Because an enormous striped beast was strolling towards the cave. Towards me and Eejit.

'I don't like the look of that,' I said.

'Oh, I do,' said Atkins, the moron. 'I love tigers.'

'That's not a standard tiger. It's one with the longest teeth since the dawn of dentists. Teeth that could do an awful lot of damage to…'

And that's when I got what Grunt had in mind for us. Thought I did anyway.

'You berk,' I said, wishing I had a hand free to slap a nearby head.

'What have I done?' Atkins asked.

'What have you done? What have you done? I'll tell you what you've done. You invented a

47

ringtone that gives apemen ideas they shouldn't have had for about fifty generations. Ideas like serving strangers up for lunch to peckish flesh-eating wild beasts.'

The sabre-tooth tiger came closer. And closer. Snarling. I started to jig again, which believe me wasn't easy, strapped to a boulder.

'If this was a story,' I said, 'one of us would be wriggling himself free right now and we'd get out of this in the nick of time. Be good to read a story like that, wouldn't it? But it's not a story, it's about as real as my life gets, so wriggling free doesn't look like being an option.'

'I dunno what you're talkin' about,' said Atkins.

'Don't worry, nor do I. This is panic speaking. Another minute, if those teeth don't get me first, I might just wet myself.'

'Me too.'

I glanced at him. 'I thought you were keen to meet that animal.'

'I am. But I didn't have a slash before they tied us up.'

'Oh, that'll look really good, won't it?' I said. 'You and me, stripped to the bone by our toothy friend there, piddle dribbling down from where our personal bits used to be. Not exactly the stuff of heroic tales, is it?'

You know, when you're fixed to a boulder with an extinct carnivore with choppers like bread knives eyeballing you, it doesn't feel like you're left with any alternatives apart from watching your life line-dance past with a sad smile on its face, or closing your eyes and screaming till it's all over. I was just getting ready to do the second of these when a bunch of screams that weren't mine got in first. They came from Grunt's ringtone-enhanced apemen as they leapt from the shadows with clubs and rocks in their hands. The tiger looked kind of shocked about this, and who can blame it? The shock didn't last, though. Before it could growl 'Hey, let's talk about this' the apemen had clubbed it to a furry pulp.

'Ah, poor kitty,' said Eejit, wiping a tear from his eye with a free hand.

'How come you've got a free hand?' I asked him.

'I've been working at it.'

'Well how about getting the rest of you free too, then freeing me as a bonus?'

'OK.'

While Eejit was getting us off the boulder the apemen set about tearing the tiger limb from bloody limb. I caught Grunt looking our way. He grinned and raised a prehistoric thumb at me. That's when I realised what had *really* happened here.

'We weren't lunch,' I said to Atkins.

'Eh? But you said—'

'We were bait, to lure the beast so Grunt's lads could jump it and make *it* lunch. I hope that tiger chokes them.'

'Yeah, gimme a Lion Bar any day,' said Eejit.

He took one out of his pocket.

'Where'd you get that?' I asked.

'It's me elevenses. Want a bit?'

He snapped the bar in two and gave me the smaller half. I nibbled it, thinking that this could be the last civilised food I'd ever get. I was thinking fondly of my mother's terrible cooking when the Little Devils phone, high on the ledge in the cave, rang for the umpteenth time.

'What made it go off this time?' I wondered.

'Maybe someone's found me number,' said Eejit hopefully.

'Here?' I said. 'At this point in time? Unlikely.'

Whatever had activated the ringtone, like last time it had a dramatic effect on the apemen. They stared at the dripping lumps of raw meat in their hands and screwed their faces up. Then a couple of them grabbed some sticks and started rubbing them together faster and faster until a trickle of smoke drifted from them. Then they stuck the sticks into a heap of dry twigs and when the twigs glowed they added more. When they'd got a real blaze going they put chunks of tiger into it. Meat began to sizzle.

'I could murder a burger,' said Atkins.

'A tigerburger,' I said. 'Yes, that'd really hit the spot.' I didn't mean it. A Lion Bar was the closest I wanted to get to munching wildlife today. 'You know what just happened, don't you, Eej?'

'Yeah, they lit a fire.'

'They worked out what fire is, and how to get one started, and that you can cook on one. They're so advanced now that they could invent the wheel any minute. Or underpants. They could sure do with some of those.'

Suddenly the phone stopped ringing, like it was saying 'My work is done'. And it was. The apemen were upgraded even further. While some of them auditioned to be the first celebrity chefs, others gathered logs and started building what looked like a portaloo. Grunt himself did nothing while all this was going on, just watched. And looked thoughtful. I could guess why. The others had scrambled another rung or two up the evolutionary ladder, but he'd shot even further up. He still didn't look much different, but when he turned to us his expression was several shades sharper than it had been. And then there was the sound that came out of his mouth…

'Sorry,' I said to him, 'but did you just… speak?'

'I believe I did,' he answered, cool as you like.

'Wow. A minute ago you could only grunt. Talk about fast-track evolution. What was that word?'

'Which word?'

'Your first.'

'Power.'

'That's what I thought. Why'd you say it?'

'It's what I feel. Coursing through me. Power and intelligence. I have no doubt that I'm the smartest person around, which means that every lesser being should serve and adore me.'

'Adore you?' I said with a sinking feeling.

'Mm. Know what? I think I should find some people to bully. Might even give world domination a shot. What do you think?'

'Good plan.' I turned to Eejit. 'See what you've started? The old rock tapping isn't enough for him any more. Now he wants to hurt people. Be a tyrant. That's just evil.'

'Evilution,' said Atkins brightly.

I flipped back to Grunt. 'This ruling the world plan. It's brilliant, a real wheeze, but kind of old-hat. Well, future-hat for you. How about starting something you can really call your own? Volleyball, say. Or…golf?'

Grunt leant towards me. 'You seem reasonably advanced yourself in your way. I might be glad of someone with a brain at my side. How would you like to be my personal assistant? You can bring the monkey.'

'His name's Atkins,' I said. 'And much as we'd love to stroll with you into the sunset singing happy songs about murder and mayhem, we're booked into I'm-a-Cretinous-Caveman-Get-Me-Outta-Here. Come on, Eej.'

'What about me Nogia?' Eejit said.

'Never mind your rotten Nogia. Let's go.'

We were about to leave when some of Grunt's men pointed out a rival species mooching across the horizon. Grunt's black eyes glinted.

'Might as well kick things off with that lot,' he said. 'Enslave them, knock 'em about a bit, show 'em who's boss. Lads! Find weapons!'

Some of them still had the clubs and rocks they'd pulped the tiger with. Others tore big bones from its carcass.

'This isn't looking too good,' I said to Eejit.

He didn't answer.

'I said this isn't looking good,' I repeated.

He still didn't answer.

I looked at where he'd been when I last checked. The space was Eejit-free. He was getting good at disappearing while I was talking to him. But this could mean only one thing. He'd gone for his phone. Which meant I had to go after him.

I slipped back into the cave.

CHAPTER SIX

'Are you completely out of your pathetic excuse for a mind?' I hissed when I found Atkins climbing the cave wall.

'I want me Nogia,' he said.

'Not as much as you want your head testing. If Grunt catches you—'

'Got it!'

He took the phone off the ledge and jumped down.

'OK,' I said. 'Now let's go before—'

'Hold!'

We froze, as you do in a semi-dark cave when a talking apeman blocks the way out.

'What are you doing with that?' Grunt demanded, eyeing the phone in Eejit's mitt.

'It's mine,' said Eejit.

'Not any more it isn't. I know what it can do. It's my key to ultimate power. Total supremacy. Hand it over.'

Atkins put the phone behind his back. 'No.'

Grunt frowned. 'Are you defying me, monkey?' Eejit nodded silently. 'Oh, well, in that case…'

Grunt leapt forward, spun him round, and grabbed the hand holding the mobile. But Atkins wasn't going to give up his car boot phone without a fight – and fight he did. The only sound during their struggle came from Grunt, whose shouts brought some of his men into the cave. With clubs, rocks and bones in their fists they looked pretty dangerous, but they hadn't evolved as much as their leader, so they didn't know what to do without orders and just stood there looking confused – until Eejit dropped the phone and it started ringing.

Grunt jumped back, eyes on the fallen Nogia. He knew that another dose of the bad ringtone would evolve him and his men further still, so he was happy to just stand there and wait to become even smarter and more ambitious. Eejit looked like he was going to seize his opportunity and pounce on the phone, but suddenly the ringtone stuttered and went all hiccuppy, and when it did that something else happened – to Grunt. His shoulders sagged, his jaw went slack, he looked at me and Atkins like he was wondering which religion we were selling, and…

…the light went out of his eyes.

The stuttery ringtone had de-evolved him. He'd gone back to the way he was when we first saw him.

And he wasn't the only one. His war band dropped their weapons and sloped out of the cave, scratching their armpits. Then, slowly, slowly, Grunt turned and went after them, grunting softly, like he had an idea that something had happened quite recently but he couldn't for the life of him remember what.

Atkins didn't care about any of this. All he cared about was his phone.

'It's broken,' he said.

He picked it up. It was still stuttering, still hiccupping.

'Broken or not,' I said, 'it's turning my brain to swede. Find the off button or I'm going ape myself.'

He started jabbing buttons at random, no more idea than previously which one stopped the ringing, and on it went, on and on and on, until I just had to make a grab for it. I almost got it too, but Eejit wasn't letting go of his phone again, and a new fight started – between the two of us this time. While we were struggling for it, the temperamental ringtone lost its stutter and started playing backwards, but we carried on fighting for it regardless, Eejit because it was his phone, me to stop it ringing. The mobile's newest crazy jingle continued, and soon it was doing my head in so much that I couldn't think or gulp or scratch or do anything except struggle blindly with Atkins, until…

'WHAT ARE YOU TWO DOING IN THERE?!'

My head cleared like a switch in my ear had been flipped. The mobile was still ringing, but I let Eejit have it back anyway. I had other things to think about all of a sudden. Like the cave we were in. It wasn't a real one any more. And nearby were five model primitives, staring out through a big glass panel at someone staring in.

Mrs Baldeagle.

Then Mrs B was marching to the door beside the display, yanking it back, storming in.

'I'LL TAKE THAT!' she bawled, ripping the

Nogia from Eejit's hand. She followed this with, 'HOW DO YOU STOP THIS THING???'

'We don't know,' I said. 'That's what we were doing, trying to stop it. We came in here so it wouldn't disturb other visitors.'

She snarled like a deranged hound, dropped the still-ringing phone into a bag slung over her shoulder, and ordered us to follow her, which we did. Outside, she slammed the door and stalked off with the reverse ringtone still playing softly in her shoulder bag.

We were about to go after her when Eejit noticed something.

'Oi, Jig.'

'What?'

'He's different.'

He pointed into the display we'd just left. At the scowling ancestor-type he hadn't wanted to meet in a dark alley. Mrs Baldeagle's long-lost uncle didn't look as scary as before. He also looked kind of puzzled, like he was trying to gather some thoughts, and failing.

I whistled. 'Those Little Devils,' I said, almost admiringly.

'What do you mean?'

'The reverse ringtone must have changed

history. For his species anyway. Pulled their evolutionary plug.'

'Yeah?'

'Yeah. Just as well it didn't affect our lot. If it had de-evolved us humans, at your present stage of development you could have been turned back into a sardine and the 21st century could be populated by orang-utans. Orang-utan teachers – imagine that. Human ones are bad enough. Still, if they handed out bananas instead of detentions…'

Suddenly Eejit gripped my arm. 'Jig!'

'Now what?'

He nodded after Mrs Baldeagle. She was going into the next room. But she was walking all sort of hunched over, arms swinging, and…

…she was grunting.

'Holy ape droppings,' I said.

'This evilution business…' Eejit said, quite thoughtfully for him.

'E-*vol*-ution,' I started to say, but stopped myself. What was the point? I looked down at him. 'What about it?'

He grinned up at me. 'It's wicked, innit.'

EDITOR'S NOTE

If you haven't previously come across Little Devils products, they are very odd things indeed. Always different, never predictable, for some reason they seem hell-bent on making Jiggy's life as difficult as possible.

Not just the present-day Jiggy's either.

In *Jiggy's Magic Balls* (the first book in a spin-off series called *Jiggy's Genes*) Jiggy d'Cuer, a 15th-century ancestor, encounters a pair of wooden balls with the word 'Little' on one and 'Devils' on the other. At first the balls seem to be working against him, but then Medieval Jiggy finds a way to make them work for him – in a rather magical way…

Kit out your bedroom
JiGGY MfCuE style!

Orchard Books are offering one lucky winner the chance to vamp up their bedroom and stock it chock-full of the best STUFF money can buy! Be the envy of all your mates if you win:

- A signed copy of every Jiggy McCue book
- 26" Sony widescreen TV
- Sony Blu-ray disk player
- Xbox 360 console
- £100 HMV voucher
(to buy Blu-ray disks or games!)
- 12-month subscription to your favourite magazine or comic

MICHAEL LAWRENCE

FANG-TASTICALLY FUNNY!
THE DAILY PRESS

Out Now!

JiGGY THE VAMPIRE SLAYER
A BLOODCURDLING CAPER!

Find loads of **JiGGY** fun at

www.**JiGGYMCCUE**.com

GAMES,
COMPETITIONS
AND A **WHOLE**
LOT MORE!

Website Discount Offer

Get 3 for 2 on all Glenn Murphy books at www.panmacmillan.com

£1 postage and packaging costs to UK addresses, £2 for overseas

To buy the books with this special discount:

1.   visit our website, www.panmacmillan.com
2.   search by author or book title
3.   add to your shopping basket

Closing date is 31 July 2011.

Full terms and conditions can be found at www.panmacmillan.com

Registration is required to purchase books from the website.

The offer is subject to availability of stock and applies to paperback editions only.

≈ panmacmillan.com

More great books by
Glenn Murphy

Do bugs have Bottoms?

Glenn Murphy received his masters in science communication from London's Imperial College of Science, Technology and Medicine. He wrote his first popular science book, *Why Is Snot Green?*, while working at the Science Museum in London. In 2007 he moved to the United States. He now lives and works in Raleigh, North Carolina, with his wife, Heather, and an increasingly large and ill-tempered cat.

Why Is Snot Green? was shortlisted for the Blue Peter Book Awards 2007, Best Book with Facts category, and the Royal Society Prize for Science Books Junior Prize 2008.

Also by Glenn Murphy

Why Is Snot Green?
and other extremely important questions
(and answers) from the Science Museum

How Loud Can You Burp?
and other extremely important questions
(and answers) from the Science Museum

Stuff That Scares Your Pants Off!
The Science Museum Book of Scary Things
(and how to avoid them)

Science: Sorted! Space, Black Holes and Stuff

Science: Sorted! Evolution, Nature and Stuff

This book has been specially written and published
for World Book Day 2011. For further information
please see www.worldbookday.com

World Book Day in the
UK and Ireland is made
possible by generous
sponsorship from
National Book Tokens,
participating publishers,
authors and booksellers. Booksellers who accept the £1 World
Book Day Token bear the full cost of redeeming it.

Do bugs have Bottoms?

and other extremely important questions
(and answers) from the Science Museum

Glenn Murphy

Illustrated by Mike Phillips

MACMILLAN CHILDREN'S BOOKS

First published 2011 by Macmillan Children's Books
a division of Macmillan Publishers Limited
20 New Wharf Road, London N1 9RR
Basingstoke and Oxford
Associated companies throughout the world
www.panmacmillan.com

ISBN 978-0-956-62767-4

3 5 7 9 8 6 4 2

A CIP catalogue record for this book is available from the British Library.

Printed and bound in Great Britain by CPI Bookmarque, Croydon CR0 4TD

The text paper within this book was donated by Abitibi Consolidated and
Paper Management Services Ltd

The paper and board used in this paperback by Hodder Children's Books
and Macmillan Children's Books are natural recyclable products made from
wood grown in sustainable forests. The manufacturing processes conform
to the environmental regulations of the country of origin.

Contents

Many thanks to

Mike Phillips, for continued illustrations
of his brilliance

Gaby Morgan and all at
Macmillan Children's Books

Deborah Bloxam-Patterson at the
Science Museum, London

Prof Alun Williams BVMS, PhD, DipECVP,
MRCVS, FHEA Chair of Veterinary Diagnostic
Pathology Department of Veterinary Medicine,
University of Cambridge

Harsimran Sekhon of the Slough
Grammar School, UK – aspiring writer and
dedicated GlennMurphyBooks fan!

Justin, Serena and Matthew Sudbury

The Murphs and the Witts

And all our friends, far and wide

Why do sweaty feet stink?

Actually, sweaty feet don't stink at all. It's the sweat-eating bacteria that live on them that smell so bad. That delightful, distinctive odour of cheesy feet is released from bugs left to grow inside your stinky socks and shoes.

Sweat-eating bacteria that live on your feet?! *Gross!*

Believe me, it gets worse. These sweat-eating bugs aren't confined to your feet. They're all over your body. The average adult has a total skin area of around 2 square metres. And upon that skin live over 1,000 species of bacteria, from up to twenty different biological families (or rather, *phyla*).

That's the most disgusting thing I've ever heard. Tell me more. What are they *doing* there?

For the most part, they're just hanging out – eating and drinking the sweat, skin oil, dead skin cells and other wastes that build up on the surface of your body. It's like one big bacterial party.

Isn't that dangerous? I mean, don't bacteria give you diseases?

Some of them do, yes. But most of the 'bug'

species that commonly live on human skin – such *corynebacteria*, *micrococci* and *staphylococci* – are pretty harmless. And even the ones that can do us harm are kept safely at bay by the solid fleshy barrier of the skin itself. Once in a while, though, they can (quite literally) get under your skin and cause problems. If you suffer a nasty cut, graze or burn, bacteria can slip in through the break in your skin's defences and form a bacterial invasion (or *infection*).

. . . and then you have to take antibiotics, right?

Well, even when this invasion does happen, your immune cells usually fight the bugs off. It's only when the immune cells fail – and the infection threatens to hang around, or spread to your bloodstream – that doctors have to attack them with antibiotic drugs. And in fact, antibiotics don't typically kill the bacteria either. They just stop them growing or feeding for a while, which gives the body's own immune cells a chance to call for reinforcements and mount a counter-attack.

So if all these bugs are feeding on our sweat, why do we sweat at all?

Sweat is a major part of the body's temperature-control system. One function of your skin is to insulate your body, and stop it from getting too hot or cold. But it also uses special structures –

like hairs and sweat glands – to control your temperature when things get a little extreme.

When your body temperature drops – such as when you're caught outside in cold weather without a jacket – hairs embedded in the skin stand up to trap a layer of warm air near the skin. This prevents heat loss from the body, keeping you warm and toasty inside. But when your body temperature rises – like when you're exercising or lounging on the beach under a blazing sun – you need to lose heat, not retain it. So sweat glands deep beneath the skin release droplets of water on to the surface through tiny tubes called *sweat ducts*. Once there, these wet droplets evaporate, taking some extra heat with them.

So sweaty skin *does* have a purpose. It helps cool your body down.

So why is it just sweaty *feet* that stink?

Well, there are a few other stinky areas I can think of ...

OK – sweaty feet and armpits, then. You know what I mean. People don't usually have stinky knees or foreheads, do they?

Good point. Well, there are a couple of reasons for that. The first is that there are two different types of sweat gland in the body – called *eccrine* and *apocrine* glands. Eccrine sweat glands are found all over the body, from the scalp to the soles of the feet. They release a clear, watery kind of sweat to help regulate body temperature. Apocrine glands are found only in your armpits and – ahem – nether regions. They produce a thick, milky, yellowish sweat rich in proteins and fats – partly to expel waste chemicals from the body, and partly to communicate your own particular odour to other people. (Other animals use these smells to attract partners, but biologists are still arguing about whether this works the same way in humans!)

Unfortunately, the rich, milky apocrine-gland sweat from your armpits is also particularly tasty to bacteria, which helpfully munch on your proteins and release stinky chemicals as waste (i.e. stinky sweat = bug farts). *This* explains why armpit sweat smells different from, say, forehead sweat. And it also explains why we tend to apply deodorants (chemicals that mask or absorb stinky sweat smells) to our armpits, but not our foreheads.

That still doesn't explain why *feet* stink . . .

You're right, it doesn't. Or why some people's feet are stinkier than others. The simple answer to that one is this: some people sweat more than others (adults and teenagers, for example, sweat more than children), and some people – frankly – wash their socks more than others.

While the eccrine-gland sweat released from your feet isn't particularly tasty to bacteria, if there's enough of it the bugs will still bring the party to your trainers. If several days' worth of foot-sweat is trapped in the warm, cosy confines of an unwashed pair of socks or trainers, then the bacteria build up, and their stinky, cheese-smelling waste products build up along with them. And since some people sweat more than others, some people – and I'm not saying it's you, necessarily – should change their socks more often. At least, if they want to avoid being called Captain Reekyfeet . . .

Get it sorted: sweaty stuff

* The average adult has almost *3 million* sweat glands, which are found more or less everywhere on the body except for the lips and nipples.
* In a tropical climate, you can sweat 2-3 litres of water every hour!
* Sufferers of the disease *Chromohidrosis* have malfunctioning sweat glands which produce multicoloured sweat, in shades including red, blue, green, yellow and black.

Why don't snakes blink?

Because they don't have eyelids! Or rather, they don't have *movable* eyelids. Instead, they have transparent scales over each eye. These protect their eyes like a pair of goggles.

Snakes wear goggles?

In a manner of speaking, yes. Although unlike us, they can't take their goggles off.

Weird. Does that mean they can swim?

Well, yes. As a matter of fact, almost all snakes can swim. (Most of them can climb too. So if you're ever trying to escape from one in the jungle, don't dive into a river or climb a tree!) But that isn't really why they evolved their scaly goggles. Or why they lost their eyelids in the first place.

Wait – so snakes *had* eyelids once? Now I'm really confused . . .

Don't be. It's simple, really. Look at it this way – what are eyelids for?

Errr, I dunno. Keeping your eyes clean? Helping you sleep?

Partly, yes.* Eyelids protect eyeballs, keeping them

---

* Although you don't need to close your eyes to sleep. Many animals with eyelids – including lions, tigers and wolves – are quite capable of sleeping with one or both eyes open. Even humans do it. Well,

moist and free of dirt, grime and harmful bacteria. Fish don't have eyelids (just picture the lifeless, doll-like stare of a shark), because they don't need them to keep their eyes moist and well washed underwater. But frogs, newts and salamanders do. Millions of years ago, when fish began emerging from the seas and evolving into amphibians, they found themselves in dirty, gritty air that could dry out their eyes and blind them, making it hard to hunt or avoid being hunted.

But a few mutant ones with extra flaps of skin above or below their eyes did a little better in the new, airy environment. These eye-flap mutants survived better than those with no eye-flaps at all, and over time these simple eye-flaps evolved into movable eyelids that could blink to clear dirt or stay closed to help keep the eye moist during sleep. After a while, some of those amphibians made their permanent home on the land and evolved into reptiles, like lizards, turtles and dinosaurs. Which therefore have (or had) eyelids too.

some of them, anyway. In fact, my brother sometimes falls asleep with his eyes open. Which freaks everybody out, but has never done him any harm.

Hang on a minute — aren't snakes reptiles too?

Well spotted. Yes, they are. Snakes are ancient reptiles of the serpent family.* They evolved from a single group of legless burrowing lizards which do have eyelids. But somewhere along the way, they lost them.

But why?

No one knows for sure. But many biologists think it was to make them better burrowers and hunters. Instead of closing their eyes to protect them from dirt as they burrowed – or slithered after prey through thick undergrowth – snakes evolved a permanent, see-through scale over each eye. These transparent scales – called *brilles* – allowed snakes to burrow and slither with their eyes wide open, making it easier for them to find and chase prey. And once they had evolved these handy dirt-goggles, there was little point in having eyelids any more. (Think about it – you don't need to close your eyes underwater when you're wearing goggles in the pool, do you?) So eventually, they lost their eyelids entirely.

So do these goggle-wearing snakes have good eyesight, then?

Some do. Tree snakes, for example, have very

---

* Or technically, the sub-order *Serpentes*. Latin always sounds more posh and impressive to your mates at the zoo.

good eyesight, and use it to spot prey among leafy treetops. But most burrowing snakes have pretty poor vision. And – lacking external ears of any kind – they're also completely deaf. It seems that snakes have become so good at hunting things in burrows and thick undergrowth that they no longer need their eyes or ears much to do it.

But how can they hunt if they can't see or hear anything?

Most snakes use their incredibly keen senses of touch, taste and smell to track and capture prey. While they don't have ears, their bodies and jawbones are very sensitive to vibrations coming through the ground. So they can track a scampering mouse by 'listening' for its footsteps in the earth. Some snakes – like pit vipers – can also detect an animal's body heat, using infrared sense organs behind their nostrils. In this way, they can 'see' the warm outline of a mouse's body against the cooler background of plants and rocks. A bit like those cool infrared goggles soldiers use.

So they don't just have goggles, they have night-vision goggles? Man — snakes are *cool*!

Yup. But perhaps their most important senses are the combined supersense of taste and smell. When a snake flicks its tongue out, it's actually smelling and tasting the air. The tongue samples

the air and passes it to a special organ in the roof of the mouth, called the Jacobsen's organ, which is so sensitive that a snake can taste week-old footprints in the ground, or sniff out water particles from rivers hundreds of metres away. With this, the snake builds up a kind of smell-a-vision picture of the world around it, navigating and hunting by smell and taste alone. Which can be a big advantage on a dark night.

So snakes are basically deadly ninja mouse-assassins.

Errr, well, they eat insects, frogs, birds and mammals too. But in a way, yes.

Coooooooool-ness. OK — one more question. If a snake doesn't have eyelids, how can you tell if he's asleep?

Good question. It's not easy.

One way is to watch for the tongue. If the tongue is flicking out once in a while, the snake is probably awake. If there's no tongue-flicking at all for several minutes, it's probably asleep. But then again, I wouldn't count on it . . .

Snake stuff:
top 10 facts about serpents

1 Snakes are very ancient – they've been around for over 150 million years.

2 A human backbone contains 33 bones (or *vertebrae*). Snakes have up to 400.

3 Except for sea snakes, snake skins are actually dry and smooth rather than wet and slimy.

4 Pet snakes can live in captivity for over forty years.

5 Snakes are found on every continent except Antarctica.

6 There are no wild snakes in Ireland or New Zealand.

7 Most snakes are not venomous, but a few are *seriously* venomous and can kill a healthy adult human with a single bite.

8 King cobras generally avoid humans. But if cornered, they can deliver enough venom in a single bite to kill twenty people.

9 Green Anacondas can weigh up to 250kg – more than most Grizzly Bears.

10 Black Mambas are among the fastest snakes in the world. They can slither at over 12mph (20km/h). The fastest human in the world – sprinter Usain Bolt – can hit 23mph (37km/h). So while he might be fine, the rest of us had better steer clear of angry mambas!

Why does your tummy rumble when you're hungry?

Because when your brain senses that you're hungry, it empties your stomach, squeezing out stomach gases and half-digested slop to make room for the lovely grub to come. As these gases and liquids gurgle through your guts, they create loud rumbling noises in your belly.

Really? Like gurgling drainpipes inside your body?

Exactly. Only the pipes are meaty and have more twists and turns. And they're filled with half-digested liquid food (called *chyme*) rather than rainwater.

Hmmm. It doesn't sound much like a gurgle in *my* belly. More like a growling bear or something.

That's because the sound changes as it vibrates through the muscle, meaty fibres and skin of your belly, so that by the time it gets to the outside, the sound is much lower-pitched. Technically, tummy rumbles are called *borborgymi*.* And you're right – by the time they get to the outside, they sound more like low growls than tinkly

---

* And if you say 'borborgymi' in a silly, low-pitched voice, it sounds like just like the thing it describes!

gurgles. But if you put your ear to someone's belly just as it rumbles,[*] you'll hear the high gurgly bit beneath the rumble, which you can't normally hear from a distance.

But why would you want your stomach to squeeze shut if you're about to eat something? Wouldn't you want it to stay open, so you can digest things?

It doesn't really squeeze shut. It just contracts a bit to push out the stuff that's still in there, in order to make room for more. And in fact, not much digestion goes on in the stomach at all.

Eh? I thought the stomach had acids in it that melt and digest your food for you . . .

Well, it does contain acids that break the food down a bit. And together with the churning, mashing muscles of the stomach wall, these help liquefy your food. This is partly to make digestion easier later on, but mostly so you can fit more grub in your stomach at once. The main function of the stomach is to receive mashed-up food blobs from the mouth and hold them in storage for a bit, before they're passed through the gut for digestion.

The stomach doesn't extract the nutrients from your food – that's the job of the intestines.

---

[*] Make sure you ask permission – or at least warn the person – before you do this. Otherwise you'll get some very strange looks.

The stomach is basically a big, fat holding bag in your digestive system that allows you to eat large amounts of food at once, instead of slowly grazing away all day. It evolved so that we (and other animals) can 'eat and run' – snarfing large quantities of food on the move, and keeping them in store for slow digestion later on.

OK . . . so how does your brain know you're hungry in the first place?

Basically, it senses changes in the levels of sugars and fats in your bloodstream. When levels drop too low, the brain releases clever chemical messengers (called hormones) into your blood that make you feel hungry and want to seek out food. Then, when you finally find food, it sends quicker signals (through nerves) to your mouth, stomach and gut, preparing them for fast and efficient grub intake. Often, even *looking* at food can be enough to trigger these nerve signals.

Is that why we sometimes drool and slobber when we see tasty-looking foods?

Yep. These brain-body (or *psychosomatic*) signals were discovered by a famous Russian biologist and psychologist named Ivan Pavlov. He revealed them by ringing a bell every time he fed a group of dogs. After a while, the dogs would drool at the sound of the bell alone, proving that it wasn't the food itself that was making the dogs

slobber – it was the thought of food (or rather, hearing something that made them think of food, even if the food wasn't present).

In the same way, when you haven't eaten for a while, and you're suddenly presented with a steak, cake or milkshake, you'll start to drool from salivary glands under your tongue and at the back of your mouth. As you munch and chew, the saliva starts to break down starchy bits of your food, and keeps it moist so that it slides down your food-tube (or oesophagus) more easily.

Wow. I'm getting hungry just thinking about it, now . . .

If you like, you can go even further, and do a little brain-body experiment. Try this:

Imagine you're lost in a hot, dry desert and you haven't eaten for days.

Now picture, in your mind, a huge, fat, juicy hamburger. Really see it in your mind's eye, every detail – the rich, luscious meat . . . the crunchy lettuce beneath . . . the tomato, both sweet and sour, on top . . .

Now imagine raising the burger to your open mouth . . . the smell of it wafting up your nostrils as you take a big, juicy bite . . .

Drooling yet?

Ohhhhhhhhhhhhhh. No fair. That does it – I'm off to McDonald's . . .

Have fun!

Why do your fingers go wrinkly in the bath?

Because your skin is actually an organ system made up of separate layers of tissue. Spend too long in the bath, and the dry, outer layer will expand and spread out, while the layer beneath stays put. This creates folds and wrinkles in spots where your skin is especially tight – like your feet, hands and fingertips.

Wait – skin is an organ?

Yes, it is. In fact, it's the largest organ in the body.

But I thought organs were, y'know, like big lumps of meaty stuff . . .

Well, an organ is just a collection of tissues that work together for a common purpose. And while most organs are a bit easier to play football with, that doesn't mean your skin doesn't qualify. Skin isn't just a flat, boring sheet of body tissue. It's actually very complex. It's made up of two main tissue layers – called the *dermis* and *epidermis* – and also contains other tissues like hair, nails, glands and nerve endings. Skin varies in thickness from 2 to 4mm – thinner in some places (like the knees and elbows) and thicker in others (like the soles of the feet).

The *dermis* (which is Latin for 'skin') is a rich

living layer of skin cells, blood vessels, sweat glands and oil glands. This is the pink, bloody bit that gets exposed if you manage to graze or chop off more than a few millimetres of skin in an accident. But ordinarily you never see it, as above (or outside) this lies the epidermis.

The *epidermis* (which means 'outer skin') itself contains four layers – an outer layer of hard, dry, dead skin cells that are constantly shed from the body, and three underlying layers of living skin cells that grow, divide and push upwards to replace the ones you've shed.

It's the *outer* part of the epidermis that goes wrinkly in the bath. This is because, while the cells in the under-layer are firmly attached to each other, and to the dermis beneath, the cells in the outer layer are not. So when your warm bath water is absorbed into the dry outer layer of the epidermis, it swells up, spreads out and forms ripples and wrinkles. This is mostly due to a skin protein called keratin, which helps to keep the tough, outer layer of skin waterproof. When it's dry, keratin forms wide flat sheets. But when

it absorbs water, the protein twists and folds in on itself, creating wrinkles in the sheets.

But why doesn't that happen all the time — like every time you wash your hands?

Because ordinarily your epidermis is kept oily and waterproof by proteins and oil glands in the dermis. But if you spend too long underwater (and especially in warm water), the oil gets washed out, and water begins to seep in. The longer you stay in the bath, the more water is absorbed, and the wrinklier you get.

So if you stayed in there long enough, would you end up looking like an old granny? Or a big pink raisin?

Thankfully, no. There's only so much water your skin can absorb, so there a limit to how wrinkly you can get.

That's a relief. So is that what skin is for, then? To keep water out?

Actually, it's designed to keep water in, rather than out. Since your body is 60–75% water, it has to keep as much of it in as possible – only allowing out small amounts through sweat, tears and urine. So the tough, oily barrier of your skin helps prevent your body from dehydrating. And as an organ system, skin does loads of other useful jobs within the body.

Like what?

Well, it's not just a barrier to water. It also forms a fleshy shield against bacteria, viruses and other nasty microbes. It protects our bodies from harmful chemicals and radiation. It stores fat and water, which help to insulate the body against extreme temperatures, and it helps to control our inner body temperature, using hairs and sweat glands to trap and release heat.

Wow! Skin is pretty clever stuff.

That's not all! Skin is also a huge sense organ, and without it you'd have serious trouble figuring out what the world around you was up to. Nerve endings embedded in your skin sense temperature, pressure and pain, and they work together to give you your sense of touch. Without it, you'd have serious trouble walking and picking things up, let alone running, dancing, writing, drawing, or playing video games. And believe it or not, skin even helps with digestion and nutrition.

What!? How?

For starters, your skin uses sunlight to produce vitamin D, which helps you to absorb nutrients, such as calcium. The skin helps you get rid of things too. While body wastes and toxic chemicals are mostly peed and pooed out of

your body, they're also sweated out through your skin. Your skin can even absorb some medicines that help to keep you healthy. Ever seen those medicine 'patches' people slap on their arm? Well, it's through capillaries (tiny blood vessels) in the skin that these drugs and medicines are taken into the bloodstream. In the future, more and more of our medicines might be delivered this way, rather than in pills and injections.

But you can't actually *eat* through your skin, right?

Right. Sadly, most food particles are too large to get through. And even if you could absorb food through your skin, your immune cells would probably just attack the undigested food blobs once they made it into your bloodstream, thinking they were dangerous bacteria. So while slapping beef stew on like suntan lotion might be fun, it won't do you much good.

It might, however, make you very popular with your dog ...

Why do cats hide their claws but dogs don't?

Because dogs *can't* retract their claws – even if they want to – as their paws and claws are built differently from those of cats. And for good reason. While dogs basically only need blunt claws for digging, cats need sharp, retractable claws to stalk, thrive and survive.

Wait – so dogs can't actually retract their claws at all? Not even a bit?

Nope. Their doggy paws just aren't built for it. Like most other mammals, cats and dogs have 'finger' bones within their paws, called *phalanges*. Each claw-tipped 'toe' on the paw contains three phalange bones. We humans have phalanges too, in our hands and feet. If you look at your own hand, with your fingers outstretched, the phalanges are the bones that lie between your knuckles and finger joints. You have three phalanges in each finger (except for the thumb, in which the middle phalange bone is missing). Same goes for the feet. There are three phalanges in each toe (although they can be harder to spot compared with the ones in the fingers).

OK . . . so what makes a cat's phalanges different?

In humans, gorillas, dogs and most other mammals, the three phalanges are very similar to each other in shape (they just get a little smaller and thinner as they get closer to the tip of the finger or toe). But in cats, the final 'toe-tip' phalange – the one with the claw attached – is a different shape to all the others, and is attached to the phalange behind it by three or four special fleshy bands or *ligaments*. (For us, it would feel a bit like having four elastic bands looped between our knuckles, only the bands would be less stretchy.)

When the cat's paw is relaxed (with its toes curled under, like a loose fist), the ligaments above the phalanges remain short and tight, holding the claw up and back. But when the cat's paw is flexed (with its toes held out straight, like the fingers of a flat, open hand), the ligaments below the

phalanges tug on the base of the final 'toe-tip', levering the claw forward and down. So when it wants to use its claws to scratch, the cat extends and spreads the 'fingers and toes' on each paw. As soon as it relaxes and folds them again, the claws retract. This helps cats keep their claws sharp when they're not in use, preventing them from being ground down with each padding footstep, as dogs' claws are.

But wouldn't having sharper claws help dogs too? Like, make them better at hunting and defending themselves?

Not really, no. Because cats and dogs hunt (and fight) in very different ways. When hunting, dogs (and related species like wolves, hyenas and dingoes) tend to work in packs, chasing down their prey at a steady run. When their prey becomes too exhausted to escape or fight back, they move in for the kill with snapping jaws and teeth. Blunt claws give dogs grip while running and help them to dig and bury any bits of meat or bone they want to save for later. But sharp claws wouldn't do these jobs any better.

Cats, on the other hand, tend to hunt alone. And in general,* they prefer the stealthy, stalk-

---

* There are, of course, a few exceptions to this. Lionesses hunt in packs, and cheetahs are partial to high-speed chases. But most cats really can't be bothered with that kind of thing. And even lionesses and cheetahs sneak as close as possible to their prey before they unleash the final charge.

and-pounce method to a lengthy chase. Feline hunters like to approach their prey quietly, getting as close as possible before they make their move. Then they spring forward with claws outstretched, tripping up their prey and pinning them to the ground, and finish 'em off with a swift and deadly bite to the neck.

So you see now why cats need to be able to retract their claws. On the sneaky, stalking approach, keeping the claws inside their soft, padded paws helps muffle their footsteps, and prevents the clicking or scrabbling noises their claws would otherwise make. Then, when they pounce, claws kept sharp inside their fuzzy feet help them to snag and hold down struggling prey. Plus, of course, they make very handy weapons in a cat-scrap. Corner an angry kitty (or, for that matter, lion, tiger or leopard), and you'll soon see the claws come out.

Is that it, then? Cats hide their claws to keep them quiet, and to keep them sharp for attacking?

Well, there's one more reason why cats like to keep their claws sharp. *Climbing*. While very few dogs* can climb at all, almost *all* cats are good climbers. Some – like leopards and jaguars – are *phenomenal* climbers. They

---

* Some, like the Singing Dogs of New Guinea, can and do climb trees. But they're a rare exception to the general, doggy rule.

practically *run* up trees, rather than claw their way up them. Leopards even drag their kill up into trees to protect it from non-climbing scavengers like wild hunting dogs and hyenas. Wild dogs and wolf packs make formidable fighters and foragers. But when it comes down to agile hunting and deadly attacking . . . you can't beat a silent, sneaky cat.

So dogs are like tough, hard-nut hunting gangs, while cats are like ninja assassins — who strike without warning and slip away into the night . . .

Something like that, yes.

Coooool. I wish I was a ninja-cat assassin. You know what? That would make a great video game . . .

What?

Think about it — *Ninja Cat Assassin 3D*! You could stalk rats and mice, annoy the dog, trip people up on the stairs — it'd be brilliant!

Errr . . . OK . . . if you say so.

I'm calling the PlayStation people right now . . .

Facts about cats

* There are over 500 million domestic cats in the world, with 33 officially recognized breeds.
* Calico (or tortoiseshell) cats are almost always female.
* The average life expectancy for a house cat is 15 years; for a stray cat, only 3–5 years.
* Unlike dogs, cats *can* see colours, but they have trouble telling reds and greens apart.
* It's true that cats always land on their feet. Or at least, they do if they're given time to adjust in mid-air. As they fall, they do a special acrobatic twisting sequence – first the head turns towards the ground, then the upper body and front legs, and finally the back legs. With all this done, they round their back and extend their feet to lessen the impact on landing.

Those clever ninja kitties.

Why do leaves fall off trees in the autumn?

Some – but not all – trees drop their leaves in the autumn to prepare for the harsh winter to come. Dropping leaves helps some plants to save energy and water and also helps prevent them from freezing to death in low temperatures.

So trees drop their leaves on purpose?

Some do, yes.

That doesn't make sense.

Why not?

Well, how does lopping off leaves help a plant save energy? Don't plants need leaves to grow?

That's right, they do. As you've probably learned in biology at school, plant leaves are a bit like living solar panels. They use energy from sunlight to turn water and carbon-dioxide gas into sugars,* in a process called *photosynthesis*. These energy-rich plant sugars then feed their own growth – along with that of all the animals that eat the seeds, fruit or body of the plant.

---

* Plus, luckily for us, a bit of oxygen on the side. Without plants and photosynthesis, we air-breathing animals would have no air to breathe.

Yeah, I know all that. But doesn't losing leaves mean fewer solar panels, less energy and less growth for the plant? That's like chopping your fingers off to save supplying them with blood. You might save a bit of energy, but now you've got no fingers, you can't pick up any more food.

Well, yes – losing leaves does mean less growth. But sometimes that's not such a bad thing. Growing and maintaining leaves, seeds and fruit requires energy and water. Plants receive and trap their energy from sunlight and get water and nutrients from the soil around their roots. But in a harsh winter, sunlight, soil nutrients and free water in the soil all become more scarce. So if, in these tough winter conditions, the plant recklessly spends all its energy growing, seeding and fruiting, it might not survive long.

So it's less like

chopping off fingers and more like going into hibernation. In wintry climes, many animals – like squirrels, bats, bears and badgers – hibernate through the harsh winter. Rather than use up lots of energy staying warm and hunting during the coldest, leanest months, they feed up in the autumn, then sleep deeply to save energy right through the winter. Then in spring, when food becomes more plentiful, they emerge to start feeding and thriving again. When trees and plants drop their leaves in winter, they're doing much the same thing.

I s'pose that makes sense, now you put it that way. But how does dropping leaves help prevent trees from freezing? Wouldn't they stay warmer with more layers on, like winter coats on furry animals?

You might think so, yes. But again – you can't really compare the leaves of a plant with the furry coat of an animal. Fur evolved to trap warm air near the skin of mammals, keeping them toasty in cold weather. But leaves don't really serve that purpose. Leaves are basically for *trapping sunlight*, and for *exchanging gases and water*. Each leaf contains hundreds of little pores or gaps called *stomata*. The plant opens and closes these to control how much carbon dioxide comes into the leaf, and how much oxygen and water vapour are let out. In summer, this all ticks along nicely.

But in winter, the watery leaves can freeze solid, drawing heat from the body of the plant itself. And while many plants contain clever 'antifreeze' chemicals to prevent their cells being damaged by freezing, it's a much safer tactic to simply drop your watery leaves before the winter to prevent heat loss. Dropping leaves also protects some trees from becoming weighed down with heavy snowfall, which can topple the tree, damaging its trunk and roots. So there are lots of reasons to do it!

Hmmmm. OK – I get that. But there's one more thing I've never sussed out . . .

What's that?

Why do the leaves on some trees change colour before they drop off? Is it some sort of signal to the other trees, so they all know to do it at once?

No, not quite. Trees can't see each other, and – as far as we know – don't signal each other to drop their leaves. Instead, the leaf-drop (or *senescence*, as biologists call it) is usually triggered when the tree senses (using special shape-shifting proteins within the leaves) a drop in the number of daylight hours, or by a drop in temperatures below a certain level.

The reason the leaf changes colour is because of the light-trapping proteins, or *pigments*, within

the leaf. These are the same proteins that help trap energy from sunlight during photosynthesis. The main pigment is called *chlorophyll*, and it absorbs the blue and red bits from sunlight while reflecting most of the green (which is why leaves look green in the first place).

Now sometimes there are also reddish, yellowish and orangey pigments within the leaf – chemicals that absorb and reflect different bits of sunlight. But there's so much more of the chlorophyll that you can't see them. *Except*, that is, when the leaf-drop (or senescence) is triggered. When that happens, the green chlorophyll pigment breaks down first, leaving the red, yellow or orange pigments behind. Eventually, these break down too, and the leaf goes brown and falls off. But for a few days or weeks, the autumn leaves seem to burst into flame as bright red, orange and yellow leaves appear all over the place.

Who knows – on some other planet, somewhere out in Space, there might be trees with blue or purple pigments instead. Then maybe there would be bright blue tropical rainforests, and beaches lined with purple palm trees.

Wow! I'd love to see that!
Me too . . .

Do bugs have bottoms?

Yes, they do. Albeit very small, bug-sized ones. All but the very oldest and simplest animal species have bottoms. As far as Mother Nature is concerned, if you have a mouth, you need a bottom. Any other arrangement would be a recipe for disaster.

Disaster? Why?

Well, think about it – what are mouths and bottoms actually for?

Eating food. And . . . err . . . getting rid of it.

Exactly.

So if you were an animal with a mouth but no bottom, would you, like, swell up and explode or something?

Sort of, yes. Keep cramming food into a tube with only one open end, and eventually the food will either spill back out of the top, or the tube itself will split apart. Once food and water has passed your stomach, fleshy valves prevent it moving back in there from the guts (or intestines) further down. So without an 'exit' for your digested food and body wastes, poo would pile up in your intestine until the gut wall burst

or split – or you vomited it back up (and, yes, that does happen!) – allowing the bacteria from your gut to infect and poison your insides.

Ouch!

So, you see, bottoms are rather important. Which is why almost all animals – including bugs – have them.

***Almost* all? So a few animals *don't* have mouths or bottoms?**

Right. While the vast majority of animal species do have separate mouths, bottoms and food-tubes, the simplest and most ancient animal families on the planet do not. These include sponges, starfish, jellyfish and anemones. Some of these animals have no mouth and bottom at all. Others lack a *separate* mouth and bottom.

Eh? What does that mean?

It means they have their mouth and bottom in the same place – using the same, single . . . ahem . . . opening for both purposes. So I guess you could say they have a *bouth*. Or a *mottom*.

Yuck! Gross!

You asked.

Buy why is it only the *oldest* animal types that have no proper bottom?

Because – just like eyes, arms, legs and everything else – mouths, bottoms and digestive systems have *evolved* in the animal kingdom. Before the animals came bacteria and other tiny, single-celled creatures like amoebas.* When you're only one cell wide, it's simple enough to absorb nutrients from the water or air around you and immediately put them to use inside your body. This is called intracellular (or 'inside-cell') digestion, and all single-celled life forms do it.

But if you've evolved into something a bit more complex – a multi-celled animal like a sponge, flatworm, fish or ferret – then things are a little different. Now you're going to need ways of getting nutrients from the outside of your body to the bits deeper inside – to the hungry organs buried beneath layer upon layer of body cells and tissues.

Sponges – the simplest multi-celled animals – get around this with lots of little channels or cavities in their bodies, which allow tiny nutrient

---

* Actually the correct word for more than one amoeba is *amoebae*. Which, when correctly pronounced, rhymes with 'Phoebe'. This makes me wonder what would be the correct name for a group of girls all called Phoebe . . .

molecules from the water around them to pass deep into their bodies. Once inside these *digestive cavities*, the nutrients are absorbed and digested inside the cells, much as they are in bacteria.

So do jellyfish and starfish have these cavities too?

Jellyfish, starfish and anemones go one better. Since they have to eat larger food morsels (like plankton, crabs and small fish) they have a *digestive duffle*. This is a big fleshy bag inside their bodies, within which their prey is broken down by acids and digestive juices. This done, they absorb the nutrients and allow the rest to fall out, along with any other wastes from their bodies. So the opening to the digestive duffle – usually surrounded by arms or tentacles – works as both a mouth *and* a bottom. And you could say it either has both, or neither.

Ahh – now I get it. So what was the first animal with a mouth *and* a bottom? You know, in two different places. Separate, like.

That would have been something like a flatworm. Active, complex animals like worms, crustaceans and insects were the first animals on the planet to evolve a food-tube – otherwise known as a *digestive tract*. In worms, this tract is just a simple tube running from an opening at the head end

(the mouth) to an exit at the back (the bottom*).

In prawns, lobsters and crayfish, it's the tube that runs along the back of the animal, where you'd expect the spine to be. This is often mistaken for a blood vessel or 'vein', and when chefs chop them out to make seafood taste better, they say the prawn or shrimp has been 'de-veined'. They're quite wrong, of course. It's not a vein at all – it's the digestive tract, filled with fishy-smelling prawn poo. Like all invertebrates, these animals have no backbones, and their guts run down their back (or dorsal) side.

In vertebrates (animals with backbones), the digestive tract runs along the belly, rather than the back. Newts, frogs, cats, dogs, hippos, horses, humans and other vertebrates have food-tubes that are up to ten times longer than their bodies, coiled up inside to save space. These super-long guts give more surface area for absorbing nutrients, and have specialized pouches and organs for storing food and making digestive juices. This allows vertebrates to eat larger chunks of food at once, to digest tougher food sources and to survive for longer periods without eating.

So worms, prawns, bugs, snakes, spiders and frogs all have bottoms too?

Correct.

---

* Or as biologists call it, the *anus*. Which comes from the Latin word for 'ring'.

One more question, then —

What's that?

What does bug poo _look_ like?

Well, a bit like ours. Only _much_ smaller . . .

Gut stuff: facts about digestion

* The largest digestive tract on Earth belongs to the Blue Whale. An adult Blue Whale's gut can be up to 250m (830 feet) long, and is wide enough for a child to swim through.
* Hyenas have among the most powerful digestive systems of all animals, which allows them to scavenge body parts that other animals cannot eat. Their powerful jaws help them pulverize and swallow and digest the hardest bone. Only teeth, hair and horns are brought back up, undigested.
* In snails and other molluscs, the digestive tract is twisted around inside the shell, leaving their bottoms situated above their heads.

Why is the sky blue?

Simple, really. Because the sky is just loads of air stuck to the planet, and air is not see-through – it's blue.

Eh? Wait a minute – I thought air was invisible . . .

Ah, there's the thing, see. Small amounts of air *are* pretty much clear or transparent (and just very, very slightly bluish). So it *seems* like air is invisible. But if you get a big chunk of air in one place and try to look through it, you see that all that 'slightly bluish' adds up to a very real and obvious blue colour. And that's what we see in the sky: a massive layer of air, made of billions and billions of very slightly blue air molecules, giving us a beautiful sky-blue . . . er . . . sky.

Is that it, then? The sky is blue because air is a bit blue?!

Pretty much. Same thing goes for the water in lakes and oceans: they look blue because water isn't colourless either – it's very slightly blue. Look down through thousands of tonnes of it and it looks blue, but scoop out a glass of it and it looks clear. That's why the thin layer of seawater that washes on to the beach with each wave is clear, but the ocean itself is blue.

But I heard the sea is blue because it's reflecting the sky . . .

Sorry – lots of people (including some teachers!) say this, but it simply isn't true. Think about it: haven't you ever seen a blue sea under a cloudy white or grey sky? Exactly. The sea might not look as *bright* a blue colour on cloudy days, because less light is getting through the clouds to shine into and off the water. But it's still blue, rather than pure grey or white.

But that's simple!

Yes, it is. Of course, if you want to know why *air* is blue in the first place, then things could get really interesting . . .

Go on, then.

People often use the words 'air' and 'oxygen' as if they mean the same thing. But while there is plenty of oxygen in air, what we call 'air' is actually lots of different gases mixed together. This includes some weird exotic ones like xenon and argon, but it's mostly made of nitrogen (about 78%) and oxygen (about 21%). Anyway – when light from the Sun hits these gas molecules, some of the light goes straight through them, and some of it gets absorbed by the molecules and thrown back out again. Now here's the tricky bit: the light from the Sun is white, but white light actually contains all the colours of the rainbow –

something scientists call the *spectrum* of visible light. (Isaac Newton showed us that a few hundred years ago by using glass shapes to split it up.)

OK . . .

Colours all look different to us because they all have different *frequencies*. Don't worry about what *frequency* means for now – it's enough to know that the blue-green end of the light spectrum has a higher frequency than the red-orange end. So yellow light has a higher frequency than red light, green is higher than yellow, blue is higher than green, and so on.

Erm . . . my brain hurts . . .

Stick with it – we're nearly there. Now, remember those gas molecules in the air? Well, they tend to absorb and scatter only the high-frequency (or the green and blue) bits of the light that hit them; the low-frequency (red and orange) bits go straight through. So as light from the Sun comes through the air in the Earth's atmosphere, the blue bits of it get scattered a lot more than the red bits. These blue bits get scattered all over the sky so seem to come from everywhere when we look up at it. Hence, the big blue sky.

Got it. But what about sunsets? Then the sky looks red . . .

At sunset (and sunrise too), the Sun is low on the horizon. When this happens, the light from it has to cut diagonally through the atmosphere (instead of straight down and through, as it does when the Sun is right overhead). This means the light has to come through more air than usual before making it to our eyes. More air means more scattering – and even the red bits get lobbed about this time. So before the Sun's rays are hidden from us at sunset, and just as they start to appear at sunrise, we're treated to a fiery skyful of scattered red light.

Why is snot green?

Basically, because it's the result of a fight between nasty bugs and body cells that make a green-coloured goo.

What?!

Seriously. Snot is made of a sticky substance produced inside the nose that traps and flushes out harmful bacteria. These nasty bugs try to get up your nose when you breathe them in. The sticky stuff stops them getting down your throat and into your lungs, and it also contains cells that your body produces to fight and kill the bugs. It's these that make the green goo. Sneezing and blowing your nose help to clear it all out.

Ugh. Fine. But what do they make the green goo for?

The body cells form part of the incredibly clever and complex defence system in your body. They make special proteins called *lysozymes*, which help them bust open, eat and digest the bacteria – a bit like the acid in your stomach. For this reason, we call the cells *phagocytes*, which is Latin for 'eaty-cells' (which you may prefer, but biologists use 'phagocytes' because it sounds more important and clever). It's one of these bacteria-busting proteins that has the green colour.

But why green, and not blue or purple?

This is purely because the protein contains a form of iron that reflects green light and absorbs all the other colours. Incidentally, you find a similar protein in wasabi, the type of horseradish you eat with Japanese sushi, which is why that's green too. Think about that next time you eat horseradish. Or a bogey.

I don't eat bogeys. I don't even pick my nose.

Of course you don't. No one does. No one rolls them up and flicks them, or sticks them under the desk either.

That's right. But if someone did ... why would the bogey change colour to dark green, brown or black?

That's because once it's out of its warm, moist home in your nose, the snot begins to dry up as water from it evaporates into the air. When this happens, the phagocytes die and the greenish proteins within them break up – removing the green colour from the bogey.

After this, bacteria in the air settle on to the bogey and start to eat it (waste not, want not, as my mum always says). They chew up all the

bits of phagocyte, dead bacteria and skin cells found in the snot, until all that's left is a dried-up mass of brownish-black protein leftovers. And even that gets eaten eventually.

Hang on a minute – how did you know bogeys change colour if you never pick your nose?

Oops.

Top 10 places to stick a bogey

1 Under a table
2 Under your chair
3 Under your tongue
4 On the wall
5 On a friend
6 In someone's pencil case
7 In someone's lunch
8 Behind a steering wheel
9 Behind your head
10 Back up your nose again

Why do people from different countries look different from each other?

Actually, people from different countries look pretty much the same. The differences that do exist – like skin colour and eye shape – are due to where our ancestors lived, and how they spread out from Africa and across the world.

But people *do* look different. And it seems like the further away they live from each other, the more different they look, right?

Well – sometimes, I guess. It's true that Chinese and Korean people look more similar to each other than, say, Chinese and African people do. But it's not where people live that makes them different.

What d'you mean?

Imagine this. Let's say I lined three average-looking white kids up next to each other, like a police identity parade – an American, an Australian and a South African. Assuming I didn't let them talk, could you pick out which one was which?

Probably not.

Right. And they're from different continents.

But that's cheating. They could all look the same because their families all came from the same part of Europe.

OK. So maybe it's not where you live now, but *where your ancestors came from* that makes you look different. Those three guys might look the same because their ancestors were all average-looking white Europeans.

All right, then — why do white Europeans, Chinese people and Africans all look different from each other?

Ahh – now we're getting somewhere. Good question. The short answer is this: their ancestors all started out in Africa, looking like Africans. But as they split off into groups and travelled across the globe, the descendants of the Chinese and Europeans gradually changed in appearance as they adapted to their new homes.

I don't get it.

Well, the only real difference between white Europeans and black Africans is their skin colour. Years ago, average-looking white European scientists used to tell us that this was because Africans

started out perfectly white (like them), but were tanned black by the sun. But they had it completely the wrong way round – in fact, those very same scientists (or rather, their ancestors) started out with black skin and became pasty as they moved northwards out of their homeland in Africa. This, it turns out, is due to vitamins.

What, those things you eat to stay healthy?

Yes, kind of. Vitamins are things your body needs to stay healthy, and we usually get them through food (and, more recently, pills). But your body can also make some vitamins for itself. Your skin can make vitamin D, which is important for healthy bones and teeth, but it needs plenty of sunlight to do so. In sunny regions, black skin lets through just enough sunlight to make vitamin D while also blocking the parts of sunlight that cause skin cancer. But in less sunny areas further north (or south), black skin blocks too much sun to allow vitamin D to be made properly. So the black African ancestors of white Europeans got pastier as they moved out of Africa and settled further north.

So what about Chinese people and African people? Why do they look so different from each other?

Well, the ancestors of the Chinese and other

Asian people also became paler as they moved northwards (and eastwards) out of Africa, for the same reason. The only other notable difference between Africans, Europeans and Asians is the shape of their eyes and eyelids. Asians tend to have more almond-shaped eyes, and have an extra fold of skin (called an *epicanthal fold*) on their eyelids. It is thought that this narrowing and shielding of the eyes evolved to help protect the ancient settlers of Asia from the blinding effects of the snows and winds of the mountains and plains. Some of them then passed this trait on to their Inuit and American Indian descendants, who crossed the land bridge from Asia to America thousands of years ago.

Is that it? We're all the same?

Yes.

And the only reason people look different at all is because of a bit of weather and a vitamin?

Exactly.

Kind of makes you wonder why we didn't figure all that out sooner.

Yep. It certainly does.

How loud can you burp?

The loudest burp on record is around 105 decibels – louder than a motorbike or chainsaw, and loud enough to cause real pain to anyone close enough to it. But don't try these at home, as they could be dangerous!

Louder than a motorbike?! No way!

Yup. The world-record burp measured 104.9 decibels (decibels, or dB for short, are the units used to measure volume). And that was from over 2.5m away! Close up, the World Champion burper claims to be able to reach 118dB or more. The average motorbike roars away at around 90dB – a full twenty-eight units lower!

So who did it?

An English guy called Paul Hunn. He smashed the previous burping record in July 2004, and no one has topped it yet.

How could he burp so loud?

Well, like all sounds, burps are just waves of air pressure, and, if you make these waves big enough, any sound can become loud. To create a sound, an object – like a bell or guitar string – is made to vibrate back and forth very fast by striking it, plucking it or rubbing something

against it. In turn, the object compresses the air molecules around it, making waves or vibrations that are carried through the air. When they reach your ears, these pressure waves vibrate your eardrums. From there, the vibrations are amplified by a set of little bones, picked up by a set of tiny hairs in your

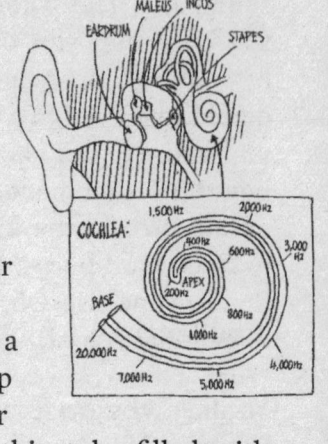

cochlea (which is a long, thin tube filled with fluid and lined with hairs – all coiled up like a snail shell in your inner ear). Here the vibrations are finally translated into nerve signals that your brain interprets as sounds, such as 'bell', 'guitar string' or whatever.

But what about burps?

In the case of burps, the vibrating object is a fleshy flap called the cardia, which closes off the stomach from the food-tube, or *oesophagus*. When air is swallowed (either by accident while you're eating, or on purpose if you're trying to force a burp), it gets trapped in the stomach. As the stomach fills with food, liquid and gas, the pressure builds up and the air bursts through the flap – vibrating it on the way out and creating that deep, satisfying BRRRRRRRRRRRRRRPPPPP

sound as it goes. Of course, if you want to *force* the burp out, you can squeeze your stomach by contracting your stomach muscles and diaphragm (which is the flat sheet of muscle underneath your stomach and lungs). This is how Mr Hunn made his burp so loud. Millions of kids around the world use the same method to force loud burps. He's just much better at it than anyone else. Oh, and he also swallowed lots of fizzy drink first.

Yeah — why *do* fizzy drinks make you burp like that?

They're made bubbly and fizzy by adding carbon dioxide gas under pressure. So when you drink the drink, you swallow the gas. The gas builds up in your stomach, annnnd . . . you can figure out the rest.

Is it dangerous to make yourself burp like that?

Well, drinking lots of fizzy drinks isn't very good for you, and swallowing air on purpose won't do your stomach any good, but that's not really what makes burping as loud as Mr Hunn does dangerous. It's after the burp leaves the body that it becomes a danger to you and others.

But if a burp is just air and sound, how could it be dangerous to anyone?

If they're loud enough and at the right frequency, sounds can be very powerful and dangerous. Ever hear of opera singers who can shatter glass with their voices alone? Well, that's true. All they have to do is hit the right pitch, and sing the note loud enough, and the glass will vibrate and shake itself to pieces. And the US military have even developed a 'sound weapon' that fires waves of air pressure and sound instead of bullets. The Vortex Ring Gun shoots a ring of vibrating air that can knock down a grown man over 10m away.

So if you burped loud enough, could you crack a person's glasses? Or knock a bunch of people over? That'd be sweet!

Err ... no. Not quite. Even the most accomplished burper, like Mr Hunn, couldn't produce enough air pressure to knock someone down. And his

burps are too low-pitched to crack glass. But he could burp loud enough to hurt your ears, or even damage them permanently.

What, really?

Yup – really. Mr Hunn burps at between 105 and 118 decibels. 85 decibels is enough to temporarily damage your hearing. Builders using pneumatic drills (which thump away at around 120dB) wear ear defenders to avoid getting hearing damage. If you burped at 165dB, that would be the same as a gunshot going off right next to your head. So burp this loud and you could deafen yourself and other people!

Yeah, and what a let-down too.

Why's that?

Just think — you can burp as loud as a gunshot, but after the first time no one can hear it. Not even you.

Err . . . yeah . . . that'd be a real tragedy.

Just one more thing . . .

What's that?

Do Brussels sprouts make you burp?

I don't . . . think so, no. Why do you ask?

They should do. Cos they come from Belch'um.

Oh *man*, that was bad.

Heh, heh. BUUUURRRRRRRRRRRPPPPP!!!!

Sci-facts: noisy stuff

The volume of a sound wave is related to its air pressure, and measured in decibels (dB). On the decibel scale, zero decibels marks the softest sound most people can hear (although some people can hear sounds at −10dB or lower). Here's how some common (and uncommon) noises measure up:

dB	Sound
0	rustling leaves
20	whisper
40	light rainfall
75	washing machine
90	motorbike
110	chainsaw, rock concert
115	one of Paul Hunn's burps (at close range)
130	jet aeroplane (from 30m away)
165	shotgun